Manage with Intention

Practical Insight for Purpose-Driven Management

By Samuel Vazquez Jr

Table of Contents

1. **Introduction**
    - Overview of Managing with Intention
    - My Leadership Journey
2. **Chapter 1: The Shift to Managing with Intention**
    - Embracing Purposeful Leadership
    - The Effectiveness of Managing with Intention
    - Keeping It Simple
3. **Chapter 2: The Foundation of Trust**
    - Why Trust Matters
    - Building Trust from Day One
    - Practicing Transparency
    - Maintaining Trust Through Consistency
4. **Chapter 3: Emotional Intelligence and Leading with Heart**
    - Understanding Emotional Intelligence
    - Recognizing and Responding to Emotional Cues
    - Leading with Empathy
    - Developing and Refining Your Emotional Intelligence

5. **Chapter 4: Transparency and Authenticity**
    - The Importance of Transparency
    - Leading with Authenticity
    - Practicing Transparency
    - Consistency in Leadership

6. **Chapter 5: Setting Goals with Intention**
    - The Simplicity of Intentional Goal-Setting
    - Aligning Goals with Values
    - SMART Goals: A Framework for Success
    - Involving the Team in Goal-Setting
    - Reviewing and Adjusting Goals

7. **Chapter 6: Intentional Hiring and Team Building**
    - The 70/30 Split: Why Soft Skills Matter Most
    - Practical Skills: The 30% That Complements the 70%
    - Hiring with Urgency and Pride
    - The Importance of the Interview Process
    - Creating a Strong Dynamic and Productive Team

8. **Chapter 7: Leading by Example**
    - The Influence of Your Actions
    - Modeling the Soft Skills You Value
    - The Role of Accountability and Servant Leadership
    - Setting Clear Expectations
    - Consistency: The Backbone of Leading by Example

9. **Chapter 8: Navigating Change with Intention**

- The Reality of Change
- Leading Through Change
- Flexibility and Adaptability
- The Role of Resilience
- Intentional Change Management

10. **Chapter 9: Intentional Time Management**
    - Why Intentional Time Management Matters
    - Setting Priorities: Focus on What Matters Most
    - The Weekly Time Management Planner
    - Consistency in Execution
    - Balancing Flexibility and Structure

11. **Chapter 10: Building a Culture of Feedback**
    - The Importance of Feedback in Leadership
    - Creating a Feedback-Friendly Environment
    - The Start Stop Continue Method
    - Incorporating Feedback into Daily Routines
    - Handling Negative Feedback with Humility

12. **Chapter 11: Intentional Conflict Resolution**
    - Understanding the Role of Conflict in Team Dynamics
    - Setting the Stage for Intentional Conflict Resolution
    - The Conflict Resolution Checklist
    - Leading with Humility During Conflict
    - Transforming Conflict into Growth Opportunities

13. **Chapter 12: Developing a Strategic Vision**
    - The Importance of a Strategic Vision
    - Crafting Your Vision: Aligning with Purpose
    - Communicating the Vision: Bringing It to Life
    - From Vision to Action: Setting Strategic Goals
    - Tracking Progress with Agile Practices

14. **Chapter 13: The Art of Effective Delegation**
    - Why Delegation Matters
    - Identifying What to Delegate
    - Communicating Clearly and Setting Expectations
    - Supporting Your Team Without Micromanaging
    - Building a Culture of Trust Through Delegation

15. **Chapter 14: Continuous Learning and Adaptation**
    - The Importance of Continuous Learning
    - Adapting to Change
    - Embracing a Growth Mindset
    - Conclusion: The Journey of Continuous Improvement

16. **Chapter 15: The Power of Intentional Consistency**
    - Why Consistency Matters
    - Understanding Your Team's Expectations
    - Leading with Consistent Actions
    - Building Trust Through Consistency

17. **Chapter 16: The Power of Managing with Intention**

- Tying It All Together: Leading with Purpose
- Why Managing with Intention Is Essential for Long-Term Success
- Final Thoughts: The Impact of Intentional Leadership

18. **Epilogue: Leading with Intention—A Lifelong Journey**
    - Reflecting on Your Leadership Journey
    - The Power of Managing with Intention
    - A Call to Action

Introduction

Have you ever wondered why some managers inspire unwavering loyalty and dedication from their teams, while others struggle to maintain basic engagement or even gain respect? The difference doesn't lie in the tasks they manage but in how they intentionally interact with the people they both directly and indirectly lead.

My name is Samuel Vazquez, and over the past 20 years, I've had the privilege of leading teams across various industries. Early in my career, I realized that the most successful teams weren't just well-managed—they were intentionally managed. This revelation changed my approach to leadership, transforming my role from a task manager to a leader who drives meaningful engagement and long-term success. I wanted to simplify something that is actually quite straightforward when done correctly and intentionally.

So, what does it mean to manage with intention? It's about making deliberate choices in how you lead, focusing on building trust, fostering open communication, and ensuring that every decision aligns with your team's and organization's goals and best interests. It's the difference between reacting to situations and proactively shaping outcomes. It's about being genuine in your interactions and consistently showing up for your team in a way that inspires confidence and respect.

This book is a collection of my personal insights and strategies developed throughout my career—lessons learned from both successes and challenges. My goal is to provide you with practical tools and actionable advice that you can apply to your own leadership journey. Whether you're new to management or looking to refine your skills, this guide will help you lead with purpose and intention. I've stripped away the unnecessary complexity that many people add and made the concepts easily digestible and simple to implement.

Throughout this book, we'll explore the key attributes of intentional management, from building trust and transparency to developing emotional intelligence and resilience. We'll dive into real-world examples from my career journey, share actionable tips, and discuss why the human touch in management is irreplaceable—even in the age of AI and automation. We'll also touch on managing with intention during the recruiting and hiring phases, as this is a prime opportunity to build a dynamic team. Additionally, we'll discuss the importance of looking for specific attributes and skills when hiring for management or leadership positions that have direct and indirect impacts on employees, ensuring long-term success and creating an organization where people feel valued, respected, and trusted.

I invite you to join me on this journey of managing with intention. As you read, think about how you can apply these principles and simple strategies to your own leadership role. The goal is not just to manage but to lead with intention, making a lasting impact on your team and organization.

Chapter 1: **The Shift to Managing with Intention**

When I first started my career in management over 20 years ago, I was often overwhelmed by the sheer volume of theories, strategies, and best practices that were supposed to guide me as a leader. I found myself constantly disagreeing with how others were doing it and, based on my own experiences being managed, I knew I wanted to be different and simplify what I believed was a broken and over-complicated strategy in organizations. This transformed into what I now refer to as managing with intention.

Managing with intention, as I've come to define it, is all about leading with purpose. It's about making deliberate choices that align with both the goals of my team and the broader mission of the organization. It includes being authentic, non-judgmental, and personable. Rather than just reacting to challenges as they arise, I learned to take a proactive approach, considering the impact of every decision I made. This shift in perspective was transformative, not just for me, but for the teams I've had the privilege to lead.

I realized early on that managing tasks was only a small part of the job. The real work—and the real reward—came from leading people with intention. This means being fully present and engaged with my team, understanding that every interaction, no matter how small, contributes to the overall success of the group. Whether I was setting goals, giving feedback, making them feel appreciated, or addressing conflicts, I made it a point to approach each situation with a clear purpose in mind.

Why It's Effective

I've seen firsthand how managing with intention can change the dynamic of a team. When I began to lead with intention, I noticed a significant shift in how my team responded to challenges and to each other. They became more engaged, more motivated, and more aligned with the goals we were working toward. They felt valued and personally invested in the overall success of the team and organization.

I'll never forget one of the most pivotal moments in my career. I was brought in to manage an established team that was struggling with low morale, frustration, and high turnover. They were hitting our deadlines, but something was clearly off. The energy was low, behaviors were negative, and it felt like they were just going through the motions. I took a step back to observe and analyze the current state of the business.

Next, I leaned into my principles and knew I needed to act with intention. I met with the team individually and collectively to hear their concerns and ideas on how we can improve the experiences and perceptions they've acquired during their time on the team. Simple action, right? The next thing I did was listen. No judgment, no interruptions. I just listened to them. You'd be surprised how those two simple steps can change so much about how they feel in a positive way. Together, we came up with a plan to move forward. My promise to them was I would listen more, involve them in decisions, and make sure they understood how their work contributed to the bigger picture. Reignite that fire inside them. Gain agreement.

The results were almost immediate. Not only did morale improve, but I also saw a noticeable boost in productivity, and the turnover rate dropped significantly. The approach I took with them was strategic and, most importantly, intentional. This will contribute to an environment where people feel valued, respected, and motivated to do their best work. Long-term vs. in the moment.

Keeping It Simple

One of the things I've learned about managing with intention is that it doesn't require a complex set of tools or strategies. In fact, simplicity is one of its greatest strengths. By focusing on clear, straightforward actions, I've found that I can lead more effectively and with less stress.

For example, I always start by setting clear expectations for both myself and my team. I ask myself, "What are the key outcomes we want to achieve, and how can I communicate these goals in a way that everyone can understand?" By simplifying the process, I make it easier for my team to follow my lead and stay aligned with our objectives.

Consistency is another important aspect of managing with intention. Over the years, I've found that being consistent in my actions and decisions builds trust within the team. When my team knows what to expect from me, they feel more secure and are more likely to bring their best selves to work every day.

Conclusion

Managing with intention has been a game-changer for me, both personally and professionally. By focusing on simple, deliberate actions, I've been able to create positive, productive environments where teams can thrive. As we move forward in this book, I'll share more of the strategies that have worked for me—building trust, fostering transparency, and developing the emotional intelligence needed to lead with intention. Remember, while managing people should be simple in theory, it takes intention to make it truly effective. And that intention starts with you.

Chapter 2: The Foundation of Trust

If I had to pinpoint the single most important element of effective leadership, it would be trust. Trust is the foundation upon which all successful teams are built. Without it, even the most talented group of individuals will struggle to perform at their best. Trust doesn't just happen; it must be cultivated and maintained through intentional actions and consistent behavior.

From the outset of my leadership journey, I knew that trust was something I had to give before I could expect to receive it in return. Unlike other leaders and managers who expect you to earn their trust, I give 100% of my trust to my teams on day one and challenge them to keep it. This approach shows that I have confidence in them and their ability to do the work they were hired to do, in a way that fits them and their styles, while staying within process and guidelines.

Why Trust Matters

Trust is the glue that holds a team together. It's what allows team members to feel safe enough to take risks, share ideas, and admit when they need help. When trust is present, people are more likely to collaborate, communicate openly, and support each other. On the other hand, a lack of trust can lead to a toxic work environment where people are afraid to speak up, innovation is stifled, and productivity suffers.

In my experience, teams that operate in an environment of trust are more resilient, more creative, and more effective. They're able to navigate challenges and setbacks more easily because they know they can rely on each other. This is why I prioritize building and maintaining trust from the very beginning of my relationship with any team.

Building Trust from Day One

As I mentioned earlier, I start by giving my team 100% of my trust on day one. This is a deliberate and intentional act that sets the tone for our working relationship. By showing that I trust them, I'm also showing that I respect them and believe in their abilities. This initial trust creates a positive feedback loop—when people feel trusted, they're more likely to act in ways that reinforce that trust.

But trust isn't something you can just give and then forget about. It requires ongoing effort to maintain. One of the ways I do this is by being transparent in my actions and decisions. I make it a point to communicate openly with my team about what I'm doing and why I'm doing it. This not only helps to build trust but also ensures that everyone is on the same page and working towards the same goals.

Practicing Transparency: The Key to Sustaining Trust

Transparency is one of the most powerful tools for building and maintaining trust. When you're transparent, you're not only sharing information but also showing that you have nothing to hide. This fosters a culture of openness and honesty, where people feel comfortable speaking up and sharing their thoughts.

In my leadership roles, I've always made it a priority to be transparent about my decisions, especially when it comes to difficult or unpopular choices. I explain the reasoning behind my actions and make sure that my team understands the bigger picture. This doesn't mean that everyone will always agree with me, but it does mean that they'll trust that I'm making decisions with their best interests in mind.

Transparency also means showing humility in times of crisis and admitting when you don't know something. I've found that being honest about what I don't know but committing to finding the answer and getting back to the team, strengthens trust. It shows that I'm human, that I value their input, and that I'm committed to solving problems collaboratively.

Maintaining Trust Through Consistency

Consistency is another crucial factor in maintaining trust. People need to know that they can rely on you to act in a certain way, regardless of the circumstances. This doesn't mean being rigid or inflexible, but it does mean being consistent in your principles and in how you treat others.

For example, if I say that I value open communication, I make sure to model that behavior consistently. I listen to my team's concerns, provide regular updates, and encourage open dialogue. When people see that I'm consistent in my actions, it reinforces their trust in me as a leader.

Conclusion

Trust is the foundation of any successful team. By giving trust freely, practicing transparency, and maintaining consistency in your actions, you can build a strong foundation that will support your team through any challenge. Remember, trust is not something that can be demanded or forced; it must be earned through intentional and consistent behavior. As you continue to lead with intention, make trust your top priority, and you'll see the positive impact it has on your team and your organization.

Chapter 3: **Emotional Intelligence and Leading with Heart**

From the beginning of my leadership journey, I understood that emotional intelligence (EQ) was crucial—something that was often missing in many of the managers I encountered early in my career. These managers lacked self-awareness and the ability to connect on a real, genuine level. They often came across as judgmental and unauthentic. I made a promise to assert my EQ when in a leadership role and lead by example.

Emotional intelligence is about more than just managing emotions; it's about recognizing and understanding the emotions of others and using that awareness to manage relationships effectively. When you lead with heart, you connect with your team on a deeper level, creating an environment where people feel valued, respected, and understood.

Why Emotional Intelligence Matters

Emotional intelligence is a key component of managing with intention. It allows you to navigate the complexities of human relationships and create a positive, supportive work environment. When leaders lack emotional intelligence, they may struggle to build trust, handle conflict, or motivate their teams. On the other hand, leaders with high EQ can inspire loyalty, foster collaboration, and drive better performance.

In my experience, the most effective leaders are those who are not only aware of their own emotions but also empathetic towards the emotions of others. They understand that emotions are an inherent part of the human experience and that they play a significant role in how we work and interact with others.

Recognizing and Responding to Emotional Cues

One of the most important aspects of emotional intelligence is the ability to recognize and respond to emotional cues. This means being attuned to the emotional undercurrents in the workplace—the subtle signs of stress, frustration, or disengagement that can impact team dynamics.

In the early days of my career, I saw how ignoring these emotional cues could lead to breakdowns in communication, conflicts, and a decline in morale. I made a conscious effort to not only manage my own emotions but also to respond to the emotional needs of my team members. This wasn't about being soft or letting emotions drive decisions; rather, it was about acknowledging that emotions are a natural part of the workplace and that they can't be ignored.

By paying attention to these emotional cues, I was able to address issues before they escalated and create a more supportive and cohesive team environment. This, in turn, led to higher engagement, better collaboration, and improved performance.

Leading with Empathy

Empathy is at the core of emotional intelligence and is one of the most important traits of an intentional leader. When you lead with empathy, you show that you genuinely care about your team members as individuals, not just as employees. This fosters a culture of trust and openness, where people feel comfortable sharing their ideas, concerns, and feedback.

Leading with empathy means putting yourself in your team members' shoes and considering their perspectives. It means listening actively, without judgment, and responding in a way that shows you understand and value their experiences. This doesn't mean you have to agree with everything they say, but it does mean that you acknowledge their feelings and take them into account when making decisions.

In my leadership roles, I've always made it a point to lead with empathy, especially during times of change or uncertainty. I've found that when people feel heard and understood, they're more likely to be engaged, motivated, and committed to the team's goals.

Developing and Refining Your Emotional Intelligence

Emotional intelligence is not a fixed trait; it's something that can be developed and refined over time. Here are some practical steps you can take to enhance your EQ and lead with heart:

1. **Practice Self-Awareness:**

   - Take time to reflect on your own emotions and how they impact your behavior. Recognize your triggers and learn to manage them effectively.

2. **Cultivate Empathy:**

   - Make an effort to understand the perspectives and emotions of others. Listen actively and show that you value their experiences.

3. **Enhance Your Communication Skills**:

   - Communicate with clarity, compassion, and authenticity. Be mindful of your tone and body language, as they can convey as much as your words.

4. **Manage Stress and Conflict:**

   - Develop strategies for managing stress and resolving conflicts in a constructive way. Stay calm under pressure and approach challenges with a positive mindset.

5. **Seek Feedback:**

   - Ask for feedback from your team on how you can improve your emotional intelligence. Use this feedback to make adjustments and continue growing as a leader.

Conclusion

Emotional intelligence is a critical component of managing with intention. By leading with heart, you can create a positive, supportive environment where people feel valued and motivated to do their best work. Remember, the most effective leaders are those who are attuned to the emotions of their team members and who use that awareness to build strong, trusting relationships. As you continue your leadership journey, make emotional intelligence a priority, and you'll see the positive impact it has on your team and your organization.

Chapter 4: **Transparency and Authenticity**

In an era where trust in leadership is paramount, transparency and authenticity have become non-negotiable elements of effective management. As leaders, we are constantly scrutinized—not just by the results we deliver but by how we deliver them. I've learned that when you lead with transparency and authenticity, you build a foundation of trust that withstands the pressures of change, challenges, and uncertainty.

Why Transparency Matters

Transparency is about being open, honest, and forthcoming with information. It's about creating an environment where there are no hidden agendas, and where people feel they are kept in the loop about decisions that affect them. Transparency fosters trust, which is the bedrock of any strong team.

In my leadership roles, I've seen how transparency can prevent misunderstandings, reduce anxiety, and increase alignment within a team. When people feel informed, they're more likely to be engaged and committed to the team's goals. Conversely, when transparency is lacking, it can lead to speculation, mistrust, and disengagement.

The Importance of Authenticity

Authenticity, on the other hand, is about being true to yourself and your values. It's about leading in a way that is consistent with who you are, rather than trying to conform to an external idea of what a leader should be. When you lead with authenticity, people can sense that you are genuine, and this builds a deeper connection and trust.

Early in my career, I made a conscious decision to lead with authenticity. I recognized that trying to be someone I wasn't, or trying to lead in a way that didn't align with my values, was not only exhausting but also ineffective. By embracing who I am and leading in a way that feels true to me, I've been able to build stronger, more trusting relationships with my teams.

Practicing Transparency: The Key to Sustaining Trust

Transparency isn't just about sharing information; it's about how you share it. It's about being open with your team about the reasons behind your decisions, the challenges you're facing, and the goals you're working towards. It's also about showing humility in times of crisis and admitting when you don't know something. I've found that being honest about what I don't know, but committing to finding the answer and getting back to the team, strengthens trust. It shows that I'm human, that I value their input, and that I'm committed to solving problems collaboratively.

In my leadership roles, I've made it a point to practice transparency consistently. For example, during a significant organizational change, I held regular meetings to update my team on what was happening, why it was happening, and how it would impact us. I encouraged open dialogue and made sure that everyone had the opportunity to ask questions and share their concerns. This approach not only kept the team informed but also made them feel involved and valued.

The Power of Leading with Authenticity

Leading with authenticity means being honest about who you are, what you stand for, and what you expect from your team. It means showing up as the same person, regardless of the circumstances, and being consistent in your actions and decisions.

One of the ways I lead with authenticity is by being transparent about my own challenges and struggles. I've found that when I'm open about my own experiences, it encourages others to be open as well. This creates a culture of vulnerability and trust, where people feel safe to share their own challenges and seek support.

Authenticity also means leading with integrity—making decisions that align with your values, even when it's difficult. In my career, I've faced situations where I had to make tough decisions that weren't popular, but I knew they were the right thing to do. By staying true to my values and leading with integrity, I was able to maintain the trust and respect of my team.

Consistency: The Bridge Between Transparency and Authenticity

Consistency is the bridge that connects transparency and authenticity. When you are consistent in your actions, decisions, and communication, you reinforce the trust that you've built with your team. They know what to expect from you, which creates a sense of stability and security.

In my leadership journey, I've learned that consistency doesn't mean being rigid or inflexible. It means being consistent in your principles and in how you treat others. For example, if you value open communication, you need to consistently model that behavior by listening actively, providing regular updates, and encouraging dialogue.

Consistency also means following through on your commitments. If you say you're going to do something, do it. If you can't, be transparent about why and what you're doing to address it. This level of consistency builds trust and shows your team that you are reliable and dependable.

Conclusion

Transparency and authenticity are essential components of managing with intention. By being open, honest, and true to yourself, you build a foundation of trust that strengthens your team and drives success. Remember, transparency isn't just about sharing information; it's about how you share it. And authenticity isn't just about being yourself; it's about being consistent and leading with integrity. As you continue to lead with intention, make transparency and authenticity a priority, and you'll see the positive impact they have on your team and your organization.

Chapter 5: **Setting Goals with Intention**

Setting goals is one of the most fundamental aspects of leadership, yet it's an area where many leaders struggle. Goals provide direction, motivate action, and create a sense of purpose. But not all goals are created equal. Over the years, I've learned that the key to effective goal-setting is intention—setting goals that are meaningful, aligned with your team's values, and designed to Inspire commitment and drive results.

The Simplicity of Intentional Goal-Setting

When I first started setting goals as a leader, I realized that the process didn't have to be overly complicated. In fact, I found that keeping it simple was often more effective. I focused on setting clear, achievable goals that were directly tied to our broader mission and values. This approach not only made the goals easier to understand and achieve but also helped to create a stronger sense of purpose within the team.

Throughout my career, the simplicity and intentionality of my goal-setting approach have consistently paid off. One of the most rewarding projects I led at Verizon involved restructuring our customer support operations. The project's success was due in large part to the clear and intentional goals we set at the outset. These goals were not just about meeting deadlines or hitting targets—they were about creating a better experience for our customers and improving the efficiency and morale of our team.

Aligning Goals with Values

One of the most important lessons I've learned about goal-setting is the importance of alignment. Goals that are aligned with your team's values and the organization's mission are far more likely to be successful. When people see the connection between their work and a larger purpose, they're more motivated to put in the effort required to achieve the goals.

In my leadership roles, I've always made it a point to involve my team in the goal-setting process. I believe that when people have a say in the goals they're working towards, they're more likely to be committed to achieving them. I also ensure that the goals we set are aligned with our core values, so that the work we do feels meaningful and fulfilling.

For example, when setting goals for a new project, I start by asking myself and my team, "What are our values? How can we align these goals with those values?" This might mean prioritizing customer satisfaction, fostering collaboration, or focusing on innovation. By aligning our goals with our values, we create a sense of purpose that drives us to succeed.

SMART Goals: A Framework for Success

One of the most effective tools I've used for intentional goal-setting is the SMART framework. SMART stands for Specific, Measurable, Achievable, Relevant, and Time-bound. This framework helps to ensure that the goals we set are clear, realistic, and actionable.

- **Specific:** Goals should be clear and well-defined. Instead of setting a vague goal like "improve customer service," I would set a specific goal like "reduce customer service response time by 20% within the next three months."
- **Measurable:** Goals should include criteria for measuring progress. This helps to keep the team motivated and allows us to track our progress. For example, we might measure progress by tracking the number of customer inquiries resolved within a certain timeframe.
- **Achievable**: Goals should be challenging but attainable. Setting unrealistic goals can lead to frustration and burnout, while setting goals that are too easy can lead to complacency. I always strive to find the right balance.
- **Relevant:** Goals should be aligned with the broader mission and values of the team and organization. This ensures that the work we do is meaningful and impactful.
- **Time-bound**: Goals should have a clear deadline. This creates a sense of urgency and helps to keep the team focused on achieving the goal within a specific timeframe.

By using the SMART framework, I've been able to set goals that are not only achievable but also meaningful and motivating. This has been a key factor in the success of the teams I've led.

Involving the Team in Goal-Setting

As I mentioned earlier, involving the team in the goal-setting process is crucial. When people have a say in the goals they're working towards, they're more likely to be committed to achieving them. This also helps to ensure that the goals are realistic and aligned with the team's capabilities and values.

In my leadership roles, I've always made it a priority to involve my team in the goal-setting process. I start by having an open discussion about our values, our mission, and what we want to achieve. I encourage everyone to share their ideas and perspectives, and I make sure that the final goals reflect the input of the entire team.

This collaborative approach not only helps to create more meaningful and achievable goals but also fosters a sense of ownership and accountability. When people feel that they've had a hand in setting the goals, they're more likely to take ownership of the work required to achieve them.

Reviewing and Adjusting Goals

One of the most important aspects of goal-setting is flexibility. While it's important to set clear and specific goals, it's also important to recognize that circumstances can change. As a leader, it's your job to regularly review the goals and make adjustments as needed.

In my experience, reviewing and adjusting goals is an ongoing process. I regularly check in with my team to assess our progress and identify any challenges or obstacles. If we find that a goal is no longer relevant or achievable, we make adjustments to ensure that we stay on track.

This flexibility is especially important in fast-paced or rapidly changing environments. By regularly reviewing and adjusting goals, you can ensure that your team remains focused and motivated, even in the face of uncertainty.

Conclusion

Setting goals with intention is a powerful tool for driving success. By aligning goals with your team's values, using the SMART framework, involving the team in the process, and remaining flexible, you can create goals that are meaningful, achievable, and motivating. Remember, goal setting is not just about achieving short-term results—it's about creating a sense of purpose and direction that drives long-term success. As you continue to lead with intention, make goal-setting a priority, and you'll see the positive impact it has on your team and your organization.

Chapter 6: Intentional Hiring and Team Building

In my years of leadership, one principle has consistently guided me: the foundation of a successful team is built long before the first task is assigned. It begins with hiring. Over the years, I've developed a hiring philosophy that has proven incredibly effective in building strong, dynamic, and productive teams. This approach is rooted in a simple yet powerful concept: a 70/30 split between soft skills and hard skills.

The 70/30 Split: Why Soft Skills Matter Most

When I hire, I allocate 70% of my focus to identifying candidates with top soft skills and 30% to assessing their hard skills. Why? Because while you can teach someone how to use a system or perform a specific task, you can't teach intrinsic behaviors like empathy, adaptability, drive, open-mindedness, effective communication, self-motivation, collaboration, and resilience. These qualities are either part of a person's character, or they're not. And in my experience, teams that thrive in the long term are those built on a foundation of these essential soft skills.

When I'm reviewing candidates, I'm looking for the qualities that tell me this person will be successful not just in the role but in our culture. I want people who are adaptable, collaborative, coachable, agile, empathetic, driven, passionate, loyal, and strategic. These are the people who will not only do their jobs well but will also contribute to a positive, supportive, and innovative team environment.

Practical Skills: The 30% That Complements the 70%

Once I've identified candidates with the right soft skills, I then consider their practical or hard skills. This includes familiarity with our systems, applications, and tasks, as well as their previous experience in similar fields or roles. This 30% is important, but it's not the deciding factor. I've found that if someone has the right soft skills, they can usually learn the technical aspects of the job with the right training and support.

By focusing primarily on soft skills, I've been able to build teams that are not only capable but also resilient, adaptable, and cohesive. These are the teams that can weather challenges, embrace change, and continue to perform at a high level, even in difficult circumstances.

Hiring with Urgency and Pride

Another key aspect of my hiring process is the sense of urgency and pride I bring to it. I see hiring as the first touchpoint someone will have with our company, and I want that experience to be positive and reflective of our brand. I operate with urgency, ensuring that candidates aren't left waiting for days or weeks for responses or decisions. A quality experience for candidates starts with prompt communication and a streamlined process.

When I'm hiring, I'm not just filling a position—I'm building a team that reflects our company's values and culture. I approach the hiring process with pride, knowing that the people I bring on board will be the ones driving our success. This mindset has helped me to attract and retain top talent who are not only skilled but also aligned with our mission and values.

The Importance of the Interview Process

The interview process is where I really dig into the qualities that matter most. I keep the interviews simple and short, focusing on the key questions that will help me filter out those who aren't a fit while gaining more information about those who could do the job well. I ask about specific experiences that demonstrate the candidate's adaptability, collaboration, empathy, and drive. I want to hear how they've handled challenges, worked with others, and contributed to their previous teams.

You should know as a hiring manager after your first interview who you want to hire or if you need to recast out to the pool. Keep it simple and understand that those being interviewed each have their own set of circumstances as to why they are seeking an opportunity. Show that you value their time and make the process as smooth and respectful as possible.

Creating a Strong, Dynamic, and Productive Team

By following this approach, I've been able to build teams that are not only capable but also connected, motivated, and aligned with our goals. These are the teams that perform at a high level, support each other, and drive long-term success for the organization.

One of the things I've learned is that a team's success is not just about individual performance—it's about how well the team works together. When you hire people with the right soft skills, you create an environment where collaboration, communication, and mutual support are the norm. This, in turn, leads to higher engagement, better performance, and greater satisfaction for everyone involved.

Conclusion

Hiring with intention is one of the most important things you can do as a leader. By focusing on soft skills, operating with urgency and pride, and keeping the interview process simple and respectful, you can build a strong, dynamic, and productive team that will drive long-term success. Remember, it's not just about filling a position—it's about building a team that reflects your values and culture. As you continue to lead with intention, make hiring a priority, and you'll see the positive impact it has on your team and your organization.

Chapter 7: Leading by Example—The Power of Modeling Intentional Behavior

In every leadership role I've held, one truth has always stood out: people don't just follow directives; they follow behavior. As a leader, your actions set the tone for your entire team. The way you conduct yourself—how you handle challenges, interact with others, and make decisions—becomes a model for your team members to emulate. This is why leading by example is not just a leadership style; it's an essential component of managing with intention.

The Influence of Your Actions

Early in my career, I noticed how much more powerful my actions were compared to my words. I could talk all day about the importance of teamwork, but if I didn't actively participate and demonstrate what collaboration looked like, my words would ring hollow. On the other hand, when I consistently showed up for my team, took responsibility, and worked alongside them, the impact was immediate and profound. My team became more engaged, more cohesive, and more committed to our shared goals.

Leading by example is about more than just setting a good example—it's about embodying the values and behaviors you want to see in your team. It's about being the first to step up during a challenge, showing humility when mistakes are made, and consistently acting with integrity and respect. Sometimes, it means being a servant leader, stepping in to support your team in whatever way is needed to keep things moving. Whether it's rolling up your sleeves to help with a challenging task or providing the guidance and resources necessary for success, leading by example means you're never above the work. These actions create a ripple effect, encouraging your team members to mirror these behaviors in their own work.

Modeling the Soft Skills You Value

In Chapter 6, we discussed the importance of soft skills like empathy, adaptability, and effective communication in building a strong team. But it's not enough to simply hire people with these qualities—you need to model them yourself. When your team sees you practicing what you preach, they're more likely to integrate those behaviors into their daily work.

For instance, if empathy is a quality you value, demonstrate it in your interactions. Show genuine concern for your team members' well-being, listen actively when they speak, and offer support when they face personal or professional challenges. If adaptability is crucial, be open to change and encourage your team to explore new ideas and approaches, even if they involve risk. By living these values, you reinforce their importance and make them a natural part of your team's culture.

I made it a point to lead with empathy, especially during times of organizational change. I knew that change can be unsettling, so I prioritized transparent communication and offered reassurance to my team. I made sure they knew I was available to discuss any concerns or uncertainties they had. This not only helped maintain morale but also strengthened the trust between us, making it easier for the team to navigate the transition smoothly.

The Role of Accountability and Servant Leadership

Leading by example also means holding yourself accountable and being prepared to serve your team when necessary. It's easy to demand high standards from your team, but it's far more effective to demonstrate those standards through your own actions. This means being transparent about your own mistakes and learning from them, just as you would expect your team to do.

Accountability isn't just about admitting when you're wrong—it's about taking ownership of your role as a leader. It's about being reliable, following through on your commitments, and setting a consistent example for your team. There are times when leading by example requires you to take on a servant leadership role, stepping in to support your team directly to ensure that goals are met, and challenges are overcome. When your team sees that you hold yourself to the same standards you expect from them and that you're willing to serve the team's needs, it fosters a culture of mutual respect and shared responsibility.

I remember a challenging project at Verizon where we encountered unexpected setbacks that threatened to derail our progress. As the leader, I could have placed the blame on external factors or shifted responsibility to my team. Instead, I acknowledged the role I played in the situation and focused on finding solutions. I also stepped in where needed, taking on additional tasks to help keep the project on track. By taking ownership of the challenges we faced and serving my team when required, I demonstrated that accountability and servant leadership are key parts of our work ethic. This approach not only helped us overcome the setbacks but also strengthened the team's resolve to work together and succeed.

Setting Clear Expectations

An essential part of leading by example is setting clear expectations for your team. Clarity in what is expected helps to eliminate confusion and ensures that everyone is aligned towards the same goals. When you model the behaviors you want to see, you set the standard for what is acceptable and what is not, making it easier for your team to understand what they should strive for.

At the beginning of each project or initiative, I make it a point to communicate not just the objectives but also the standards of behavior and performance that are expected. This includes being clear about deadlines, the quality of work, and the level of collaboration required. By setting these expectations upfront and consistently demonstrating them in my own actions, I create an environment where my team knows what is expected and feels supported in meeting those expectations.

Consistency: The Backbone of Leading by Example

Consistency is crucial when it comes to leading by example. It's not enough to occasionally show up as a role model; your actions must align with your values and expectations every day. Consistency builds trust, and trust is the foundation of any strong team.

One of the most important lessons I've learned is that consistency in leadership doesn't mean being rigid. It means being steadfast in your principles while remaining flexible in your approach. It's about showing up as the same leader—one who is fair, transparent, and supportive—regardless of the circumstances. This kind of consistency reassures your team that they can rely on you, which in turn encourages them to be consistent in their own work.

At JP Morgan Chase, I worked on a high-stakes project that required daily check-ins and constant communication. I made sure to consistently participate in these check-ins, demonstrating my commitment to the project and the team's success. Even when the pressure was high, I remained calm, focused, and supportive, which helped the team stay grounded and motivated.

Conclusion

Leading by example is one of the most powerful tools in your leadership arsenal. When you model the behaviors and values you want to see in your team, you create a culture of accountability, trust, and excellence. Remember, your team is always watching—they take cues from how you handle challenges, how you interact with others, and how you make decisions. By consistently leading with intention, serving your team when necessary, and holding yourself accountable, you set the standard for your team's success. As you continue to lead with intention, remember that your actions speak louder than words. Be the leader you want your team to be, and they will follow your example.

Chapter 8: **Navigating Change with Intention**

Change is inevitable in any organization. Whether it's a shift in company strategy, the adoption of new technology, or unexpected market conditions, change can be both exciting and daunting. As a leader, your ability to navigate change with intention is crucial not only for your success but for the success and stability of your team. I've seen firsthand how the approach to change can make or break a team's performance and morale.

The Reality of Change: Embracing the Inevitable

Change is often met with resistance, not because people inherently dislike it, but because it introduces uncertainty and challenges the status quo. In my early years as a leader, I quickly realized that resisting change or trying to minimize its impact was a futile effort. Instead, I learned to embrace change as an opportunity for growth—both for myself and for my team.

Leading Through Change: The Power of Communication

One of the most important lessons I've learned about managing change is the critical role of communication. When people are faced with uncertainty, they crave information. They want to understand what's happening, why it's happening, and how it will impact them. As a leader, your job is to provide that information clearly and consistently.

However, communication during times of change isn't just about sharing information—it's about listening, too. I made sure to actively listen to my team's feedback, taking their perspectives into account as we navigated the transition. This not only helped me to address specific concerns more effectively but also demonstrated that their voices were valued, which in turn helped to maintain trust and morale.

Flexibility and Adaptability: Staying Agile in the Face of Change

Another key aspect of navigating change with intention is flexibility. Change rarely follows a linear path, and as a leader, you must be prepared to adapt your plans and strategies as new information, and challenges arise. Flexibility doesn't mean abandoning your goals; it means finding new ways to achieve them in the face of changing circumstances.

Adaptability is also about being open to learning and growth. Change often brings with it new challenges that can push you and your team out of your comfort zones. Embracing these challenges as opportunities to learn and develop new skills can help your team not only survive change but thrive in it.

The Role of Resilience: Bouncing Back Stronger

Change often comes with setbacks and challenges, which is why resilience is such an important trait for both leaders and their teams. Resilience is the ability to bounce back from difficulties and continue moving forward, even when things don't go as planned.

At JP Morgan Chase, I led my team through a large change that impacted performance and morale. It was a challenging time, and there were moments when it felt like we were taking one step forward and two steps back. However, I knew that my role as a leader was to maintain a sense of optimism and keep the team focused on our long-term goals.

I encouraged the team to view setbacks as learning opportunities, and I made sure to celebrate small wins along the way to keep morale high. By fostering a culture of resilience, I was able to help the team navigate the ups and downs of the transition and emerge stronger and more united on the other side.

Intentional Change Management: A Step-by-Step Approach

Navigating change with intention requires a deliberate and thoughtful approach. Here are some practical steps that have helped me lead my teams through change effectively:

1. Communicate Early and Often:

   - Keep your team informed about changes as soon as possible. Provide clear and consistent information and be transparent about what you know and what you don't.

2. Listen to Feedback:

   - Create opportunities for your team to share their concerns and feedback. Actively listen to their perspectives and use that information to guide your decisions.

3. Stay Flexible and Open to New Approaches:

   - Be prepared to adapt your plans as new information and challenges arise. Flexibility is key to successfully navigating change.

4. Foster Resilience:

   - Encourage your team to view setbacks as opportunities for growth. Celebrate small wins and maintain a focus on long-term goals.

5. Lead with Optimism:

   - Your attitude as a leader sets the tone for your team. Stay positive and focused on the future, even when facing challenges.

Conclusion

Change is a constant in any organization, but how you navigate it can make all the difference. By leading with intention—communicating clearly, staying flexible, fostering resilience, and maintaining a positive outlook—you can help your team not only survive change but thrive in it.

Chapter 9: **Intentional Time Management**

In the fast-paced world of leadership, time is one of your most valuable resources. Managing it effectively can make the difference between a team that meets its goals and one that struggles to keep up. Early in my career, I learned that without intentional time management, it's easy to get caught up in the urgent at the expense of the important. This chapter is about how to approach time management with intention, focusing on high-impact activities that drive success.

Why Intentional Time Management Matters

Intentional time management isn't about squeezing every minute out of the day; it's about making deliberate choices on how to spend your time to maximize impact. When you manage your time with intention, you're not just getting things done—you're getting the right things done. This approach allows you to align your daily activities with your team's goals and your organization's mission.

Setting Priorities: Focus on What Matters Most

The first step in intentional time management is setting clear priorities. Not all tasks are created equal, and as a leader, it's crucial to distinguish between what's urgent and what's important. Urgent tasks demand immediate attention, but important tasks are those that contribute to long-term success.

Tactics:

1. **Time-Blocking:** Allocate specific blocks of time to focus on high-priority tasks. For example, you might reserve your mornings for strategic planning and your afternoons for meetings.

2. **The Two-Minute Rule:** If a task takes less than two minutes to complete, do it immediately. This prevents small tasks from accumulating and becoming overwhelming.

3. **Delegation:** Identify tasks that can be delegated to others. Trust your team to handle these responsibilities, freeing up your time for activities that require your unique expertise.

The Weekly Time Management Planner

One tool I've found particularly useful is the Weekly Time Management Planner. This template helps you map out your week, ensuring that you allocate time to your most important tasks while still leaving room for flexibility.

Template: Weekly Time Management Planner

- **Monday-Friday:** Start each day by listing your top three priorities. Block time for these activities and allocate time for meetings, email responses, and breaks.
- **Review & Reflect:** At the end of each day, review what you accomplished and make adjustments for the next day as needed. This daily review keeps you on track and allows for continuous improvement.

Consistency in Execution

Consistency is key to making intentional time management work. It's not enough to plan your time; you must also execute your plan with discipline. Over the years, I've found that being consistent in how I manage my time builds trust within the team. They know what to expect from me, and this predictability creates a stable work environment.

Tactics:

1. **Daily Stand-Up:** Begin each day with a brief check-in with your team to align on priorities and address any immediate concerns.
2. **Time Audit:** Periodically conduct a time audit to evaluate how effectively you're using your time. Are there activities that could be streamlined or eliminated?
3. **Accountability Partner:** Consider pairing with a colleague or mentor to help hold you accountable for how you manage your time.

Balancing Flexibility and Structure

While it's important to have a structured approach to time management, flexibility is equally essential. Unexpected issues will arise, and you need to be adaptable enough to respond without derailing your entire schedule.

Tactics:

1. **Buffer Time:** Build buffer time into your schedule to handle unexpected tasks or emergencies.
2. **Reassess Priorities:** Be willing to adjust your priorities if something more important comes up. Flexibility doesn't mean abandoning your plan, but it does mean being responsive to changing circumstances.

Conclusion: The Power of Intentional Time Management

Intentional time management is about more than just efficiency; it's about aligning your daily actions with your larger goals. By managing your time with purpose, you ensure that you're dedicating your energy to the activities that matter most. This approach not only enhances your productivity but also strengthens your leadership by demonstrating to your team the value of focus and discipline.

As we move forward, remember that time management is a skill that evolves with practice. The more intentional you are with your time, the more you'll find that you're able to achieve meaningful, lasting success.

Chapter 10: Building a Culture of Feedback

As a leader, one of the most powerful tools at your disposal is feedback. Feedback, when given and received with intention, can be a catalyst for growth, improvement, and innovation within your team. However, creating a culture where feedback is encouraged, valued, and acted upon requires deliberate effort. In this chapter, we'll explore how to build and sustain a culture of feedback that drives continuous improvement and strengthens team dynamics.

The Importance of Feedback in Leadership

Feedback is essential for both personal and professional development. It provides individuals with insights into their strengths and areas for improvement, enabling them to refine their skills and enhance their performance. For a leader, feedback serves as a two-way street—offering an opportunity to guide team members while also learning from their experiences and perspectives.

In a well-established feedback culture, team members feel comfortable sharing their thoughts and observations, knowing that their input is valued and will be used constructively. This openness fosters trust, collaboration, and a shared commitment to achieving the team's goals.

Creating a Feedback-Friendly Environment

To build a culture of feedback, it's crucial to create an environment where team members feel safe and supported in both giving and receiving feedback. This begins with setting clear expectations and modeling the behavior you wish to see.

Tactics:

1. **Lead by Example:** As a leader, consistently seek feedback from your team. This shows that you value their opinions and are committed to your own growth. When you receive feedback, respond positively, and take action where appropriate.

2. **Set Clear Expectations:** Communicate the importance of feedback to your team and establish guidelines for how feedback should be given and received. Encourage constructive, specific, and actionable feedback.

3. **Normalize Feedback:** Make feedback a regular part of team interactions rather than something that only happens during formal reviews. This can be done through informal check-ins, after-action reviews, and project debriefs.

The Start, Stop, Continue Method

One simple yet effective approach to feedback is the "Start, Stop, Continue" method. This framework provides structure to feedback discussions, making them more focused and actionable.

How It Works:

- **Start:** Identify behaviors or practices that the individual or team should start doing to improve performance or collaboration.
- **Stop:** Highlight actions or habits that are counterproductive and should be discontinued.
- **Continue:** Recognize and reinforce the behaviors that are working well and should be maintained.

Example: During a team meeting, you might say:

- "I think we should start holding weekly brainstorming sessions to generate new ideas for our project."
- "Let's stop waiting until the last minute to finalize our reports. It's causing unnecessary stress."
- "I appreciate how well we communicate deadlines. Let's continue to be clear and consistent about our timelines."

Incorporating Feedback into Daily Routines

To ensure that feedback becomes an integral part of your team's culture, it's important to embed it into daily routines and practices.

Tactics:

1. **Daily Stand-Ups:** Use daily stand-up meetings as a quick touchpoint to offer feedback on recent tasks or progress. Keep it brief but constructive.
2. **1-on-1 Meetings:** Schedule regular one-on-one meetings with team members to provide more detailed feedback and discuss their development.
3. **End-of-Week Reflection:** At the end of each week, hold a brief team meeting to reflect on what went well and what could be improved. This creates a continuous feedback loop and helps the team stay aligned.

Using the Feedback Request Form

To facilitate structured feedback within the team, consider using a Feedback Request Form. This template allows team members to formally request feedback on specific areas or projects, ensuring that feedback is timely, relevant, and targeted.

Template: Feedback Request Form

- **Request Date:** [MM/DD/YYYY]
- **Feedback Requested By:** [Name] [Role]
- **Feedback Topic:** [Specific area or behavior]
- **Feedback Received From:** [Name] [Role]
- **Feedback Summary:** [Content]
- **Action Items:** [Steps to be taken based on the feedback]

This form can be used during one-on-one meetings or as part of project reviews. It encourages team members to actively seek feedback and provides a clear record of the feedback given.

Handling Negative Feedback with Humility

Receiving negative feedback can be challenging, but it's a crucial part of growth. As a leader, it's important to handle negative feedback with humility and openness. Admitting when you don't know something or when you've made a mistake can actually strengthen your credibility and foster trust within the team.

Tactics:

1. **Acknowledge the Feedback:** When you receive negative feedback, acknowledge it without becoming defensive. Thank the person for their honesty and take time to reflect on their input.

2. **Admit When You Don't Know:** If a team member brings up an issue that you don't have an immediate answer to, be honest about it. Let them know you'll look into it and follow up with them later.

3. **Take Action:** Demonstrate that you're committed to improvement by taking action based on the feedback you receive. This shows your team that their feedback is valued and can lead to positive change.

Conclusion: The Power of a Feedback Culture

Building a culture of feedback is not an overnight process, but the effort is well worth it. When feedback is woven into the fabric of your team's daily interactions, it becomes a powerful tool for continuous improvement, collaboration, and innovation. By approaching feedback with intention, you'll create an environment where everyone feels valued, heard, and motivated to contribute their best work.

As you implement these strategies and tools, remember that feedback is a gift—it's an opportunity for growth, both for you as a leader and for your team as a whole. Keep the lines of communication open, stay humble, and watch your team thrive as a result of your intentional approach to feedback.

Chapter 11: **Intentional Conflict Resolution**

Conflict is an inevitable part of any team dynamic. As much as we might strive for harmony, differing opinions, personalities, and work styles can sometimes lead to friction. However, when approached with intention, conflict doesn't have to be a negative force. In fact, it can be a powerful catalyst for growth, innovation, and stronger relationships within your team. In this chapter, we'll explore how to manage conflict with intention, turning potential disruptions into opportunities for improvement and collaboration.

Understanding the Role of Conflict in Team Dynamics

Before diving into conflict resolution strategies, it's important to recognize that conflict itself isn't inherently bad. Conflict often arises when people care deeply about their work and have strong opinions about the best way to achieve success. While unchecked conflict can lead to resentment and disengagement, managed intentionally, it can spur creativity, bring underlying issues to the surface, and foster a culture of openness and trust.

Intentional conflict resolution involves addressing issues directly, transparently, and constructively. It's about creating an environment where team members feel safe expressing their opinions, knowing that their concerns will be heard and respected.

Setting the Stage for Intentional Conflict Resolution

To manage conflict effectively, it's essential to create a foundation of trust and open communication within your team. This begins with setting clear expectations about how conflicts will be handled and modeling the behaviors you wish to see.

Tactics:

1. **Establish Ground Rules:** Early on, establish ground rules for how conflicts will be approached. For example, agree that conflicts should be addressed directly and respectfully, without personal attacks.

2. **Foster Open Communication:** Encourage open dialogue by regularly inviting team members to share their thoughts and concerns. Make it clear that differing opinions are valued and that conflicts will be addressed promptly.

3. **Be Proactive:** Don't wait for conflicts to escalate before addressing them. If you notice tension building, take the initiative to facilitate a conversation and resolve the issue before it becomes a larger problem.

The Conflict Resolution Checklist

When conflicts do arise, having a structured approach can help you navigate the situation with intention and ensure that all parties feel heard and respected. The Conflict Resolution Checklist is a practical tool you can use to guide these conversations.

Template: Conflict Resolution Checklist

- **Identify the Conflict:** Clearly define the issue at hand. What is the conflict about? Who is involved?

- **Parties Involved:** List all individuals who are part of the conflict. Understanding everyone's perspective is key to finding a resolution.

- **Initial Meeting:** Schedule a meeting with the involved parties to discuss the issue. Set a neutral tone and emphasize the goal of finding a constructive solution.

- **Gather Perspectives:** Allow each party to share their side of the story. Listen actively, without interrupting, and acknowledge their feelings and concerns.

- **Find Common Ground:** Identify areas of agreement. Even in the midst of conflict, there are often shared goals or values that can serve as a foundation for resolution.

- **Propose Solutions:** Collaboratively brainstorm potential solutions. Encourage creative thinking and consider compromises that can address the needs of all parties involved.

- **Agree on Action:** Choose the best solution and agree on specific action steps. Make sure everyone is clear on their responsibilities moving forward.

- **Follow-Up:** Schedule a follow-up meeting to review progress and ensure that the resolution is being implemented effectively.

Leading with Humility During Conflict

As a leader, how you handle conflict sets the tone for your entire team. Leading with humility means acknowledging when you don't have all the answers, being open to feedback, and demonstrating a willingness to learn from the situation. This approach not only helps to resolve the immediate conflict but also strengthens your credibility as a leader.

Tactics:

1. **Acknowledge Your Role:** If your actions or decisions contributed to the conflict, acknowledge this openly. Taking responsibility shows your team that you are committed to resolving the issue and moving forward.

2. **Admit Uncertainty:** If you're unsure how to resolve a conflict, don't be afraid to admit it. Let your team know that you will seek out additional information or consult with others to find the best path forward.

3. **Be Open to Feedback:** During conflict resolution, encourage feedback from all parties involved. Listen carefully to their input and be willing to adjust your approach if necessary.

Transforming Conflict into Growth Opportunities

When managed with intention, conflict can be a powerful driver of growth and improvement. By viewing conflict as an opportunity rather than a threat, you can help your team develop stronger communication skills, deepen their understanding of each other, and foster a more collaborative work environment.

Tactics:

1. **Encourage Reflection:** After resolving a conflict, encourage the parties involved to reflect on what they learned from the experience. What could have been done differently? How can they apply these lessons in the future?

2. **Celebrate Resolution:** Acknowledge and celebrate the successful resolution of conflicts. This reinforces the idea that conflict, when managed well, can lead to positive outcomes.

3. **Promote Continuous Improvement:** Use conflicts as a catalyst for continuous improvement. Identify any underlying issues that contributed to the conflict and take steps to address them proactively.

Conclusion: The Power of Intentional Conflict Resolution

Conflict is an inevitable part of working with others, but it doesn't have to be a negative experience. By approaching conflict with intention, you can turn potential disruptions into opportunities for growth, learning, and stronger team cohesion.

Remember, effective conflict resolution starts with a foundation of trust, open communication, and humility. When conflicts arise, address them directly and constructively, using the Conflict Resolution Checklist as a guide. By leading with intention during these challenging moments, you'll not only resolve the immediate issue but also build a more resilient, collaborative, and successful team.

As we move forward, keep in mind that managing conflict is a skill that can be developed and refined over time. With practice, you'll become more adept at turning conflicts into opportunities for positive change, helping your team to thrive in even the most challenging situations.

Chapter 12: Developing a Strategic Vision

When I first stepped into a leadership role, I quickly realized that having a clear, strategic vision was crucial to guiding my team toward long-term success. A strategic vision is more than just a statement of goals—it's a roadmap that provides direction, inspires commitment, and aligns the efforts of everyone on the team. In this chapter, I'll share how I've developed and communicated strategic visions throughout my career, implemented agile practices to track progress, and how you can do the same with intention and clarity.

The Importance of a Strategic Vision

A strategic vision serves as a north star for your team. It defines where you're headed, why it matters, and how you plan to get there. Without a clear vision, teams can easily become scattered, working hard but without a unified purpose. Early in my career, I experienced this firsthand. At one point, I was leading a team that was extremely busy—we were always moving, always doing something. But despite our efforts, we weren't making the progress I expected. It felt like we were spinning our wheels. That's when I realized that while we were working hard, we weren't working smart—we lacked a clear, strategic vision to guide us.

Crafting Your Vision: Aligning with Purpose

Crafting a strategic vision starts with understanding the broader purpose of your team and organization. When I sat down to create my first strategic vision, I started by asking myself: "What is the core purpose of our work? What do we want to achieve, and why is it important?" These questions helped me focus on the big picture, ensuring that the vision I developed was not just a set of goals, but a reflection of our collective purpose.

Tactics:

1. **Reflect on Core Values:** Begin by identifying the core values that drive your team. These values should be the foundation of your vision. For example, in one of my roles, the core values were customer satisfaction, innovation, and teamwork. I ensured that our strategic vision was deeply aligned with these principles.

2. **Engage Your Team:** Involve your team in the vision-setting process. When I developed a new vision for a team at Verizon, I gathered input from everyone. This not only helped create a vision that resonated with the team but also fostered a sense of ownership and commitment.

3. **Keep It Clear and Concise:** A vision should be easy to understand and remember. It's tempting to make it complex, but simplicity is key. When I crafted my first vision statement, I kept it straightforward: "To be the industry leader in customer service, known for innovation and reliability."

Communicating the Vision: Bringing It to Life

Once you've developed a strategic vision, the next step is to communicate it effectively. A vision is only as powerful as your team's understanding and commitment to it. I learned early on that simply stating the vision wasn't enough—I had to make it come alive for my team.

Tactics:

1. **Tell a Story:** People connect with stories, so I often use storytelling to illustrate our vision. When I introduced a new vision at Nationwide Financial, I shared a story about a customer who benefited from our services. This story helped the team see the real-world impact of our work and how our vision would guide us in making even greater differences.

2. **Regularly Reinforce the Vision:** Repetition is crucial. I made it a point to reference our vision during team meetings, one-on-ones, and even in casual conversations. This constant reinforcement helped keep the vision top of mind.

3. **Lead by Example:** Your actions must align with your vision. I always strive to embody the values and goals outlined in our strategic vision. If the vision emphasizes innovation, I encourage creative thinking and take calculated risks. If it focuses on customer satisfaction, I ensure that my decisions reflect a customer-first approach.

From Vision to Action: Setting Strategic Goals

A vision without action is just a dream. To make your vision a reality, you need to break it down into actionable steps. This involves setting strategic goals that align with your vision and provide a clear path forward.

Tactics:

1. **SMART Goals:** When setting goals, I use the SMART framework—Specific, Measurable, Achievable, Relevant, and Time-bound. For instance, if our vision is to become the industry leader in customer service, a SMART goal might be:

"Increase our customer satisfaction score by 15% within the next year."

2. **Prioritize Initiatives:** Not all goals can be achieved at once, so it's important to prioritize. I learned this while leading a team at JP Morgan Chase, where we had to decide which initiatives would have the most significant impact on our vision. We focused on high-impact projects first, ensuring we made meaningful progress quickly.

3. **Assign Ownership:** Ensure that each strategic goal has a clear owner who is responsible for its achievement. In my experience, this clarity of ownership prevents tasks from falling through the cracks and ensures accountability.

Tracking Progress with Agile Practices

To effectively track progress and stay aligned with our strategic vision, I implemented agile practices within my teams. This approach not only allowed us to be more responsive to changes but also ensured that we were continuously making progress toward our goals.

One of the key tools I used was **Jira**—a powerful platform for tracking and monitoring progress in real time. By setting up our projects in Jira, we could break down our strategic goals into manageable tasks and user stories. This structure provided a clear path forward and allowed us to monitor progress at every stage.

Tactics:

1. **Sprint Planning:** We used agile sprint planning sessions to determine which tasks and objectives to focus on in the short term, ensuring that each sprint was aligned with our long-term vision. This allowed the team to maintain focus on what was most important while being flexible enough to adapt to new challenges and opportunities.

2. **Daily Stand-Ups:** We called these DAC calls (Daily Agility Call). Daily stand-ups were an essential part of our process, providing a regular touchpoint for the team to discuss

progress, share updates, and address any obstacles. These stand-ups kept everyone aligned and allowed us to quickly address any issues that could derail our progress.

3. **Retrospectives:** After each sprint, we held retrospectives to reflect on what went well and what could be improved. This practice of continuous improvement was key to refining our processes and ensuring that we were always moving closer to our strategic vision.

Conclusion: The Power of a Strategic Vision

A well-crafted and communicated strategic vision can be a game-changer for your team. It provides direction, fosters alignment, and inspires commitment. But remember, a vision is only as powerful as the actions taken to achieve it. By developing a vision with intention, communicating it effectively, implementing agile practices to track progress, and taking deliberate steps to bring it to life, you can guide your team toward lasting success.

In my career, I've seen firsthand how a clear vision, combined with intentional tracking and agile practices, can transform a team's performance and morale. It's not always easy, and it requires constant effort and adjustment, but the results are well worth it. As you move forward, keep your vision front and center, use the tools and techniques that work best for your team, and lead with the intention to make it a reality. This approach will not only help you achieve your goals but also create a team that is united, motivated, and ready to tackle any challenge that comes your way.

Chapter 13: The Art of Effective Delegation

One of the hardest lessons I've learned as a leader is that I can't do everything myself. When I first started in leadership roles, I often felt the need to take on too much responsibility, believing that if I wanted something done right, I had to do it myself. Over time, however, I realized that this approach was not only unsustainable but also counterproductive. Effective delegation is a crucial skill for any leader, and when done intentionally, it empowers your team, builds trust, and drives greater success.

Why Delegation Matters

Delegation isn't just about offloading tasks; it's about empowering your team members to take ownership of their work and develop their skills. By delegating effectively, you create opportunities for others to grow, while freeing yourself to focus on strategic initiatives that require your unique expertise.

I remember a specific moment during my time at Verizon when I was leading a call center team through a critical project. The workload was immense, and I found myself trying to manage every detail. It wasn't long before I realized I was stretched too thin and that the quality of my work was suffering. That's when I decided to step back, assess the strengths of my team members, and begin delegating key responsibilities. The results were immediate—team members felt more engaged and responsible for their tasks, and I was able to concentrate on steering the project in the right direction.

Identifying What to Delegate

The first step in effective delegation is identifying which tasks should be delegated and which should remain under your direct control. As a rule of thumb, I focus on delegating tasks that are time-consuming but not necessarily strategic, as well as those that are within the skill set or growth potential of my team members.

Tactics:

1. **Assess Tasks for Delegation:** Review your current responsibilities and identify tasks that can be handled by someone else. Look for repetitive tasks, tasks that others can complete more efficiently, or tasks that will provide a learning opportunity for a team member.

2. **Match Tasks to Team Strengths:** Consider the strengths and development areas of your team members. Delegate tasks that align with their skills and professional growth goals. For example, if you have a team member who excels at

data analysis, delegate the responsibility of tracking and reporting project metrics to them.

3. **Retain Strategic Oversight:** While it's important to delegate, it's equally important to retain control over tasks that are critical to your role as a leader—those that require strategic decision-making or have significant impact on the direction of the project or team.

Communicating Clearly and Setting Expectations

Effective delegation requires clear communication. When assigning tasks, it's essential to provide your team members with all the information they need to succeed, including the desired outcome, deadlines, and any necessary resources.

Tactics:

1. **Define the Scope:** Clearly define the scope of the task, including what is expected, what the deliverables are, and how success will be measured. This prevents any misunderstandings and ensures that the team member knows exactly what is required.

2. **Set Deadlines:** Establish realistic deadlines for each task, keeping in mind the workload and other responsibilities of the team member. Make sure the deadlines align with overall project timelines.

3. **Provide Resources:** Ensure that the team member has access to the resources they need to complete the task successfully. This might include tools, training, or additional support from other team members.

Supporting Your Team Without Micromanaging

Delegation is not about abdicating responsibility; it's about providing the right level of support to your team without micromanaging. This balance is critical to maintaining trust and fostering a sense of ownership among your team members.

Tactics:

1. **Offer Guidance:** Be available to provide guidance and answer questions but avoid hovering or micromanaging. Trust your team members to handle the task in their own way, as long as they are on track to meet the objectives.

2. **Monitor Progress:** While it's important not to micromanage, you should still monitor progress. Regular check-ins or updates can help you stay informed without being overbearing. Tools like Jira can be useful for tracking progress on tasks in a transparent way that allows both you and the team member to stay aligned.

3. **Provide Feedback:** After the task is completed, provide constructive feedback. Acknowledge what was done well and offer suggestions for improvement. This helps the team member grow and prepares them for future responsibilities.

Building a Culture of Trust Through Delegation

Delegation is a powerful way to build trust within your team. When you delegate effectively, you demonstrate confidence in your team members' abilities, which in turn motivates them to perform at their best. Over time, this trust builds a stronger, more cohesive team.

Tactics:

1. **Delegate Meaningful Tasks:** Whenever possible, delegate tasks that contribute to the overall goals of the team or project. This shows your team members that you trust them with important work and value their contributions.

2. **Acknowledge Efforts:** Publicly acknowledge and celebrate the efforts of team members who have successfully completed delegated tasks. This recognition reinforces the value of delegation and encourages others to take on more responsibility.

3. **Encourage Initiative:** Create an environment where team members feel comfortable taking the initiative to tackle new

challenges. When team members see that their contributions are valued, they are more likely to step up and take ownership of additional tasks.

Conclusion: The Power of Intentional Delegation

Effective delegation is not just a skill; it's a mindset. It requires you to be intentional about how you manage your time and your team's talents. By delegating with purpose, you empower your team, build trust, and create a more efficient and productive work environment.

In my own journey, learning to delegate effectively has been one of the most transformative experiences in my leadership career. It's allowed me to focus on what truly matters—strategic vision, innovation, and leading with intention—while enabling my team to grow and excel in their roles. As you continue on your leadership journey, remember that delegation is not about doing less work; it's about doing more of the right work and helping your team achieve their full potential.

By mastering the art of delegation, you not only enhance your own effectiveness as a leader but also contribute to the long-term success of your team and organization.

Chapter 14: Continuous Learning and Adaptation

One of the most valuable lessons I've learned throughout my career is that the journey of leadership is one of continuous learning and adaptation. The world is constantly changing, and so are the challenges we face as leaders. To stay effective and relevant, it's crucial to embrace a mindset of lifelong learning and to be open to adapting your strategies and approaches as circumstances evolve.

The Importance of Continuous Learning

In the early days of my leadership journey, I was focused primarily on mastering the skills and knowledge required for my role at the time. However, as I progressed in my career, I realized that being a great leader isn't about knowing everything—it's about being willing to learn, grow, and evolve continuously.

Continuous learning is essential for staying ahead of industry trends, understanding new technologies, and developing the skills needed to navigate complex challenges. It also sets a powerful example for your team, showing them that learning and improvement are ongoing processes.

Tactics:

1. **Seek Out New Knowledge:** Make it a habit to regularly seek out new knowledge. This could be through reading books and articles, attending conferences and workshops, or taking online courses. For example, when I transitioned to a new leadership role at Verizon, I made it a point to immerse myself in the latest industry research and best practices related to digital transformation.

2. **Learn from Your Team:** Your team members are a valuable source of knowledge and insights. Encourage them to share their expertise and experiences, and be open to learning from them. In my experience, some of the most valuable lessons I've learned have come from my interactions with team members who bring diverse perspectives to the table.

3. **Stay Curious:** Cultivate a sense of curiosity and a desire to explore new ideas and approaches. When faced with a challenge, instead of relying solely on what you already know, take the opportunity to explore different solutions and learn something new in the process.

Adapting to Change

Change is inevitable, and as a leader, your ability to adapt is critical to your success. Whether it's adapting to new technologies, shifting market dynamics, or changes within your organization, being flexible and responsive to change can help you navigate uncertainty and lead your team effectively.

Tactics:

1. **Embrace Change:** Rather than resisting change, embrace it as an opportunity for growth and improvement. During my time at Nationwide Financial, we underwent a significant organizational restructuring. Instead of viewing it as a disruption, I saw it as an opportunity to streamline processes and enhance our team's effectiveness.

2. **Stay Agile:** Apply agile principles not just to your projects, but to your leadership style. Be prepared to pivot and adjust your strategies as new information emerges or circumstances change. This flexibility allows you to respond quickly to challenges and capitalize on new opportunities.

3. **Involve Your Team:** When adapting to change, involve your team in the process. This not only helps them feel more invested in the changes but also ensures that you have a diverse range of perspectives and ideas to inform your decisions. During a major technology rollout at JP Morgan Chase, I actively sought input from my team to ensure that our approach was practical and well-received by those who would be using the new system.

Embracing a Growth Mindset

A growth mindset is the belief that abilities and intelligence can be developed through dedication, effort, and continuous learning. As a leader, fostering a growth mindset in yourself and your team can lead to greater resilience, creativity, and success.

Tactics:

1. **Encourage Experimentation:** Create a culture where experimentation and taking calculated risks are encouraged. When your team knows that it's okay to fail as long as they learn from the experience, they are more likely to innovate and explore new ideas. I've seen firsthand how this approach led to significant breakthroughs in process improvement.

2. **Celebrate Learning:** Celebrate not just successes, but also the learning that comes from setbacks. Acknowledge the effort and growth that comes from tackling challenges, even if the outcome wasn't as expected. This reinforces the value of learning and continuous improvement.

3. **Provide Opportunities for Growth:** Invest in the development of your team by providing opportunities for learning and growth. This could be through professional development programs, mentoring, or encouraging them to take on new challenges that stretch their abilities.

Conclusion: The Journey of Continuous Improvement

Leadership is not a destination—it's a journey of continuous improvement, learning, and adaptation. By embracing this journey with intention, you can stay ahead of the curve, navigate change with confidence, and inspire your team to reach new heights.

In my career, the willingness to learn and adapt has been a cornerstone of my success. It has allowed me to grow as a leader, to overcome challenges, and to lead my teams through times of change and uncertainty. As you continue on your leadership journey, remember that there is always more to learn, new strategies to explore, and opportunities to improve.

By fostering a culture of continuous learning and adaptation within your team, you'll not only enhance your own leadership effectiveness but also create an environment where everyone is empowered to grow, innovate, and succeed. Lead with the intention to learn, adapt, and evolve, and you'll be well-equipped to face whatever challenges come your way.

Chapter 15: The Power of Intentional Consistency

From the early days of my career, I quickly understood the value of consistency. As I transitioned into management, I made a deliberate choice to lead with intentional, consistent actions. Consistency, I realized, isn't just about maintaining routines; it's about building trust, creating stability, and ensuring that your team knows what to expect from you as a leader.

Why Consistency Matters

Consistency is foundational to effective leadership. When your actions, decisions, and communication are consistent, your team feels secure and supported. This stability allows them to focus on their work without the added stress of uncertainty. Early in my career, I noticed that some of the most successful leaders were those who were predictable in their actions. Their teams knew what to expect, which built a strong sense of trust and reliability.

When I began managing teams, I was intentional about being consistent in how I led. I recognized that my team needed a leader who was steady and reliable, someone they could count on to make decisions that aligned with the values and goals of the organization. This approach wasn't just about being predictable—it was about being deliberate in every action I took, ensuring that each decision and communication reinforced the trust I was building with my team.

Understanding Your Team's Expectations

An essential part of leading with consistency is understanding what your team expects from you. From day one, I made it a point to ask each member of my team two key questions: **"What are your expectations of me as your manager?"** and **"How do you like to be managed?"** These questions put the focus on them, giving them some control over how they are approached and ensuring that I could meet their expectations consistently.

Asking these questions allowed me to tailor my management style to each individual, while still maintaining a consistent approach across the team. It also demonstrated that I valued their input and was committed to meeting their needs as a leader. This practice not only built trust but also created an environment where team members felt supported and understood.

How to Be a Consistent Leader

Being consistent doesn't mean being rigid. It means making decisions that align with your values and the team's goals and sticking to them unless there's a compelling reason to change course. Here's how I've applied this principle in my leadership:

Tactics:

1. **Set Clear Expectations:** Early on, I made sure my team knew what I expected from them. This included everything from work standards to behavior and communication. By being clear about my expectations, I created an environment where my team knew exactly what was required of them, reducing confusion and uncertainty.

2. **Follow Through on Commitments:** One of the ways I built trust with my team was by consistently following through on my commitments. Whether it was a promise to provide feedback, a decision to support a team member's initiative, or simply being on time for meetings, I made sure my actions matched my words.

3. **Communicate Regularly:** I learned that regular communication is key to maintaining consistency. By keeping my team informed through team meetings, one-on-ones, and updates, I ensured that everyone was aligned with our vision and expectations.

Consistency in Decision-Making

Consistency in decision-making is crucial. Your team needs to know that your decisions are based on a set of principles and that you apply these principles consistently. This doesn't mean you can't adapt or change your mind when new information arises, but it does mean that your decision-making process should be transparent and fair.

Tactics:

1. **Base Decisions on Core Values:** I always make decisions that align with my core values and the goals of the team. This

approach ensures that my decisions are consistent with the overall direction of the team and the organization.

2. **Be Transparent:** When I make a decision, I explain the reasoning behind it. This helps my team understand my thought process and see the consistency in my actions.

3. **Be Fair:** I apply the same standards to everyone on my team. Consistency in fairness is key to building a culture of trust and respect within the team.

Maintaining Consistency Over Time

Consistency requires discipline and self-awareness. It's easy to slip into inconsistency when under pressure but staying consistent is crucial for long-term success.

Tactics:

1. **Self-Reflection:** I regularly reflect on my actions and decisions, asking myself if I've been consistent with my values and the expectations I've set for my team. This practice helps me stay on track and make necessary adjustments.

2. **Seek Feedback:** I encourage my team to provide feedback on my consistency. Their input helps me identify any areas where I might be slipping and allows me to make improvements.

3. **Adapt Without Losing Consistency:** While it's important to be consistent, it's also important to be adaptable. When change is necessary, I communicate the reasons behind the change and how it aligns with our values and goals, ensuring that my team understands the rationale and remains engaged.

Conclusion: The Power of Intentional Consistency

Consistency might seem simple, but its impact on your leadership and your team's success is profound. By leading with intentional consistency, you build trust, create stability, and ensure that your team is aligned and focused on achieving their goals.

Throughout my career, I've seen the powerful effects of being consistent in my actions, decisions, and communication. It's not always easy, especially in the face of challenges or pressure, but the benefits far outweigh the effort. As you continue to grow as a leader, remember that consistency is a powerful tool that can help you build a strong, cohesive, and high-performing team. Lead with consistency, and you'll find that your team is more engaged, more motivated, and more successful in the long run.

Chapter 16: The Balance Between Empathy and Accountability

As a leader, finding the balance between empathy and accountability has been one of the most challenging yet rewarding aspects of my career. Both are critical for creating a healthy, productive work environment, but they require a delicate balance to ensure that neither is sacrificed for the other.

Understanding Empathy in Leadership

Empathy is the ability to understand and share the feelings of others. In a leadership context, this means being attuned to your team's emotions, challenges, and needs. Empathy allows you to build strong, trusting relationships with your team members, which is essential for fostering a collaborative and supportive work environment.

In my experience, showing empathy means more than just listening to concerns—it's about taking the time to understand the underlying issues that may be affecting a team member's performance or well-being. For example, I once had a team member who was consistently missing deadlines. Instead of immediately holding them accountable, I first took the time to understand what was going on. After a private conversation, I learned they were dealing with a personal issue that was affecting their focus. By showing empathy and providing the support they needed, we were able to address the issue together, which ultimately led to improved performance.

The Role of Accountability

While empathy is crucial, it must be balanced with accountability. Accountability ensures that team members are responsible for their actions and that the team meets its goals. Without accountability, even the most empathetic leader can struggle to achieve results.

Accountability is about setting clear expectations, providing feedback, and holding team members to the standards that have been established. It's not about being harsh or punitive but about ensuring that everyone is doing their part to contribute to the team's success.

Balancing Empathy and Accountability

Balancing empathy and accountability requires a thoughtful approach. Here's how I've managed to strike this balance in my leadership:

Tactics:

1. **Set Clear Expectations:** From the beginning, I make sure my team knows what is expected of them. This includes both performance metrics and behavior standards. Clear expectations make it easier to hold team members accountable while also providing a framework for understanding where empathy might be needed.

2. **Personalized Approach:** Each team member is different, and I adjust my approach based on their individual needs. Some may require more empathy, while others may need a firmer hand when it comes to accountability. By asking team members how they like to be managed, I tailor my leadership style to fit their preferences, ensuring that I am both empathetic and effective.

3. **Timely Feedback:** I provide feedback regularly, not just during formal reviews. This allows me to address issues as

they arise and show empathy when needed, while also reinforcing the importance of meeting expectations. For instance, if a team member is struggling, I might express understanding of their situation but also remind them of the importance of meeting their responsibilities.

4. **Lead by Example:** I strive to model the balance between empathy and accountability in my own actions. By holding myself accountable to the same standards I expect from my team, I show that accountability is a shared responsibility, not just something imposed from above. At the same time, I demonstrate empathy by being open about my own challenges and how I work through them.

Practical Application: A Personal Example

During my time at Nationwide Financial, I led a team that was dealing with a particularly stressful project. The deadlines were tight, and the stakes were high. I knew that pushing too hard could lead to burnout, but letting up on accountability could result in missed deadlines and poor performance.

To navigate this, I started by having individual check-ins with each team member. I asked them how they were feeling about the project and what support they needed from me. This allowed me to gauge the team's emotional state and adjust my approach as needed. For some, I offered additional resources or flexibility in their work schedule. For others, I emphasized the importance of meeting our deadlines and the impact their work had on the project's success.

By balancing empathy with accountability, we were able to complete the project on time and with a high level of quality. More importantly, the team remained engaged and motivated throughout the process, knowing that their well-being was valued alongside their performance.

Conclusion: The Power of Balance

The balance between empathy and accountability is not always easy to achieve, but it is essential for effective leadership. By showing empathy, you build trust and create a supportive environment where team members feel valued. By maintaining accountability, you ensure that your team stays on track and meets its goals.

Throughout my career, I have found that this balance is key to leading with intention. It requires continuous adjustment and a deep understanding of your team, but when done correctly, it leads to a strong, cohesive, and high-performing team. As you continue to develop your leadership style, remember that empathy and accountability are not mutually exclusive—they are two sides of the same coin, both necessary for creating a successful and harmonious team environment.

Epilogue: Leading with Intention—A Lifelong Journey

As we conclude this exploration of intentional leadership, it's important to recognize that the journey doesn't end here. Leadership is not a destination but a continuous process of learning, adapting, and growing. The strategies and principles we've discussed—from managing with intention to navigating change—are tools that you can refine and expand upon throughout your career.

One of the key takeaways from my experiences is the importance of consistency in leadership. Whether you're setting goals, hiring new team members, or leading your team through change, the intentionality behind your actions sets the foundation for success. It's about more than just achieving short-term results; it's about creating a sustainable, positive environment where people feel valued, motivated, and empowered to contribute their best.

Reflecting on Your Leadership Journey

Take a moment to reflect on your own leadership journey. What are the values and principles that guide you? How can you apply the lessons from this book to your current role or future endeavors? Remember, managing with intention is not about being perfect—it's about being purposeful and deliberate in your actions, and continuously striving to improve.

The Power of Managing with Intention

Throughout my career, I've seen the transformative power of managing with intention. By focusing on what truly matters—people, relationships, and purpose—you can create teams that are not only successful but also resilient and fulfilled. The impact of managing with intention extends beyond the workplace; it influences how we connect with others, how we approach challenges, and how we leave a lasting legacy.

A Call to Action

As you move forward, I encourage you to embrace the principles of managing with intention in your own work. Be deliberate in your decisions, communicate openly, and lead by example. Whether you're facing routine tasks or navigating major changes, approach each situation with a clear sense of purpose and a commitment to making a positive impact.

Final Thoughts

As you continue your leadership journey, remember the profound impact of being intentional, authentic, and genuine in all your actions. Leadership isn't about perfection; it's about being real and purposeful in every decision you make and every interaction you have. When you lead with intention, you create a foundation of trust and respect that resonates throughout your team and organization.

Being authentic means showing up as your true self, embracing your strengths and acknowledging your areas for growth. It's about leading with integrity and being transparent with your team, even in challenging times. Genuine leadership is felt—it's the difference between just managing people and truly connecting with them.

The most effective leaders are those who remain true to their values and are consistent in their actions. By staying intentional in your approach, you ensure that every decision, every conversation, and every action aligns with your core principles. This not only drives success but also fosters a culture where people feel valued, respected, and motivated to contribute their best.

In the end, leading with intention, authenticity, and genuineness isn't just about achieving results; it's about making a lasting impact on the people you lead and the organization you serve. Thank you for being part of this journey, and I wish you continued success as you manage with intention, bringing your genuine self to every leadership challenge you face.